the extreme sports collection

rock & ice climbing

top the tower

by Jeremy Roberts

rosen publishing group's

rosen central

new york

Published in 2000 by The Rosen Publishing Group, Inc.
29 East 21st Street, New York, NY 10010

Copyright © 2000 by The Rosen Publishing Group, Inc.

First Edition

Library of Congress Cataloging-in-Publication Data

Roberts, Jeremy.
    Rock and ice climbing! Top the tower/ Jeremy Roberts.
      p. cm. — (Extreme sports collection)
    Includes bibliographical references and index.
    Summary: Introduces the sports of rock and ice climbing, describing the history, equipment, safety tips, and outstanding performers.
    ISBN 0-8239-3009-2
    1. Rock climbing—Juvenile literature. 2. Snow and ice climbing— Juvenile literature.
[1. Rock climbing. 2. Snow and ice climbing.] I. Title. II. Series.
GV200.2.R63 2000
796.52'23—dc21

                        99-32892
                             CIP

contents

Mt. Blanc

A Word of Caution

Climbing rocks and ice is very dangerous. Even though some forms of the sport—such as bouldering—do not require safety equipment, it should not be attempted without experienced supervision. Although we all climb things from time to time, rock and ice climbing is not to be taken lightly.

This book is not intended as an instruction manual. Anyone interested in participating in the sport should find a qualified instructor.

What's Extreme?

Let's get something straight: What's extreme to you might not be extreme to the next person. And what's extreme to that person might be tame to you. You see, "extreme" is relative. It's something different for everybody.

For some people, nothing is more extreme than dangling by themselves off the face of a mountain or an ice wall, hundreds of feet above the ground,

held there only by their skill, their courage, and a sturdy rope. For rock and ice climbers, the most extreme activity is to climb—and the more difficult, the higher, and the faster the climb, the better. In other words, the more extreme.

Today there are the X Games, a sort of miniature Olympics for extreme sports. Athletes from around the world gather for this event to show just how extreme they can be. They climb ice walls, race down slippery, snow-covered ski slopes on mountain bikes, and jump out of airplanes with skateboards strapped to their feet. They compete to see who can grab the biggest air, who can hit the highest speeds, and who can perform the most difficult stunts. The winners are given gold medals and the title of "Most Extreme Athlete on the Planet." At least, that is, until the next X Games, when new athletes redefine what it means to be extreme.

Another version of extreme sports takes place behind the scenes, away from the glory that comes with television coverage and cheering crowds. These athletes prefer to play alone, with only nature and the elements for company. They're the mountain climbers, the backcountry bikers and snowboarders, the explorers. They'll never get a gold medal for what they do, and they probably wouldn't want one anyway. They're doing what they do because they love it, not because it attracts a crowd.

Most people agree that for a sport to be extreme, it has to be difficult—at least for the beginner. It must require specialized skills and techniques. It also requires an adventurous attitude—the kind of attitude that says there are no limits. Whether this means doing a flip off a halfpipe wall, blasting down a rocky chute of a remote mountain, or just getting on the chairlift for the first time, it all depends on who you are and what you're willing, or not willing, to try.

Extreme sports can be dangerous, but being extreme doesn't mean being foolish or taking unnecessary risks. No snowboarder wants to risk an injury that might mean never boarding again. You can be extreme and still follow safety rules.

If you think you want to be extreme but you're not sure where to start, try rock or ice climbing. You'll find an adventure with every turn. With rock or ice climbing, you can be as extreme as you want to be.

Extremely Interesting

To your left, the countryside stretches out in waves of green and brown. To your right, a crystal blue lake ripples gently with the breeze. And when you look straight ahead, all you see is rock.

You are more than 5,000 feet up on a sheer vertical rock face. To get here, you've climbed over a narrow overhang and muscled up a long crack. Now you're standing on a ledge less than two inches wide. Your hands grip narrow rounds of stone.

"On belay!" shouts your partner below. It's the signal you've been waiting for. Your safety rope is just loose enough to let you move easily. Dusted with chalk to keep them dry, your fingers stretch toward a narrow crack in the rock above. Your right hand inches in. Now you move your left hand and get a friction hold nearby. You pull upward, struggling to get a good foothold.

It isn't easy. You groan with the strain. Your left hand starts to slip.

Not a good place to slip, you think.

Luckily, you're able to push your fingers together and hang on. Your thighs strain against the stretchy material of your shorts as you toe up to a crevice. You edge your right foot in. The right shoe seems to glue itself to the rock.

So does the left. You made it.

You hear something nearby and turn your head to look.

A red-tailed hawk glides on a thermal air current. It passes by so close that you can look it straight in the eyes.

Climbing may be the most individual of sports. Going up rock or ice, every climber has a different style. There seem to be countless ways to put finger to stone or lever an axe into ice.

Climbing is also a team sport. A free climber's life is in his or her partner's hands. That's pretty extreme.

It's also rock-solid fun. Like participants in other extreme sports, climbers like to live on the edge. Climbing is a new sport, full of danger and excitement. For some climbers it's a way to keep in shape on the weekends. For others it has become almost a way of life. Hangdogs and rock hounds hang out together even when they're off the mountains or out of the gym. They have their own language and way of dressing. In fact, many of today's popular fashions, like fleece and microfibers, were first worn by mountaineers and other climbers.

The sport began with explorers blazing trails up mountains and across Arctic wastes. Then came the free climbers—daring individuals stoked by the challenge of

Mt. E

erest

sheer rock and gravity. Today sport climbing is extremely popular. Thousands of people head to gyms and rocks every day of the week. At the X Games, some of the best sport climbers compete on man-made courses. They flail up the competition tower, barely pausing to get a grip.

From bouldering to mounting an expedition to conquer Mount Everest, climbers face a range of challenges as vast as the planet.

Climbing is one sport that definitely dates back to the cavemen. Look at the spots where cave paintings have been found. You'll see that our ancestors were serious athletes, cramming and jamming every day.

As sports, rock and ice climbing do not quite go back to the cavemen, of course. Their roots lie in the Age of Exploration.

As Western civilization moved out of Europe, adventurers mapped lands and territory that their countrymen had never seen before. Often they dis-covered mountains, steep rock faces, and vertical ice in their way. Usually the early explorers went around these obstacles. If they could not, they tried to take the easiest path through or over them.

As people became familiar with the rest of the world, some adventurers decided to take the mountains head—and fingers—on. These climbers went up rock not because it was in the way to somewhere else, but for the challenge and thrill of the climb—for the sport of it. Sportsmen pitted themselves against the Alps in Europe. Two French mountaineers scaled Mont Blanc, Europe's highest peak, in 1786. In North America, mountaineers attempted to climb the Rockies out West and the Appalachians back East. By the early nineteenth century, climbing clubs were very popular in Europe. Much exploring and at least some climbing with ropes was taking place in America around the same time. But it was not until the twentieth century that climbing caught on in a big way.

Early climbers had only one goal—to get to

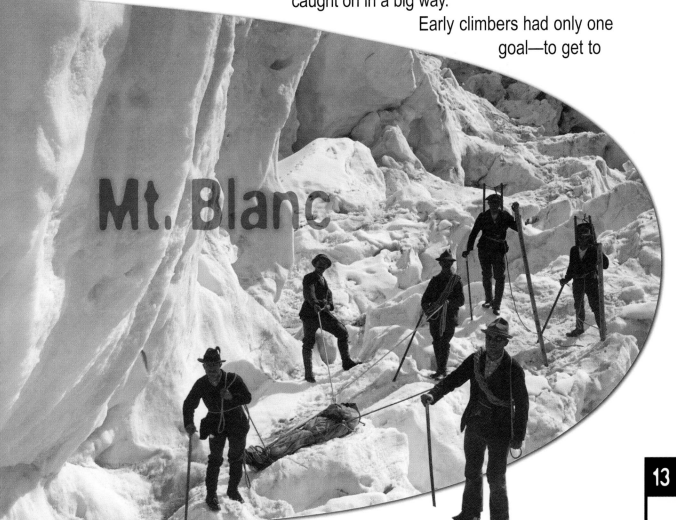

Mt. Blanc

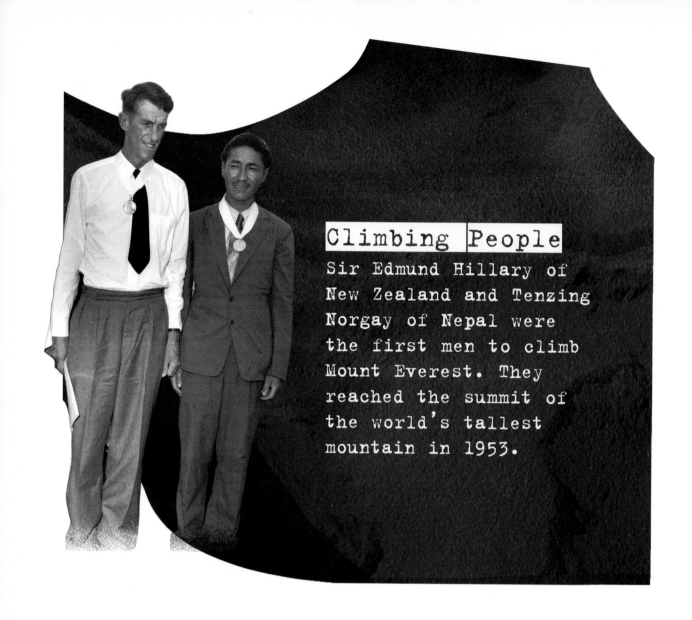

Climbing People

Sir Edmund Hillary of New Zealand and Tenzing Norgay of Nepal were the first men to climb Mount Everest. They reached the summit of the world's tallest mountain in 1953.

the top, ideally before anyone else did. Then many adventurers discovered that they simply liked the thrill of climbing. The challenge was its own reward. They sought out spots just because they were hard to climb. Vertical rock faces—*vertical* in this case means "straight up" and just a little scary—became special challenges. It did not matter that a mountain had already been climbed. In fact, the same rock face could be climbed again and again. For each person the challenge was fresh.

Free Climbing

Gradually "free climbing" became a sport of its own. In free climbing, a climber uses his or her hands and legs to get up a rock face. Nothing is supposed to help the climber—not ropes, not ladders, and definitely not helicopters.

Of course, free climbing can be very dangerous. To protect themselves, climbers use a "belay system" for safety. The system includes a rope, anchors placed in the rock, and a harness. (The rope is used strictly for safety—as a way to protect the climber in case of a fall—not as a way to advance up the rock.) Improvements in this system, especially the anchors placed in the rocks, made the sport more popular.

Sport and competition climbing are part of the free climbing family. Some sports historians say that modern sport climbing began after a group of

European climbers visited Yosemite National Park in California in the 1970s. There they saw American free climbers in action. The Europeans took American techniques and came up with some new twists.

One was to "top climb." Starting from the top of the mountain, climbers would rappel down the rock face. As they went, they would place anchors for their protection. The climb itself would then start from the bottom. The protection was left in place for other climbers. These climbers would then simply attach their ropes to the permanent anchors.

This may not seem like much, but it led to big things. With good protection already in place, climbers could concentrate on speed and difficulty. They focused on just the "technical" part of the climb. Sport climbing—and competition—was born.

Sport and Competition

Sport climbing lets more people join the fun. In some ways, it is a lot easier than the older "classic" styles. For one thing, climbers do not have to learn about placing and recovering protection. The equipment also costs less. Still, sport climbing is extremely challenging. Many of the awesome moves made by sport climbers these days would not even have been tried fifty years ago.

Women have been part of climbing nearly from the start, but they got into the sport big-time in the 1970s and '80s. Changes in the anchors and other tools helped. So did sport climbing. Social changes that led to new opportunities for women were important also. During that time more women became interested in sports and athletics. Because climbing was so individualistic, it was open to anyone. When women tried it, many liked the challenge. They also found that climbing does not require the

Climbing People

Katie Brown won three consecutive X Games gold medals before she even turned eighteen. Rated as one of the best women sports climbers in the world, she specializes in difficulty events.

Though Brown is only five feet tall and weighs just eighty-five pounds, she has an outstanding weight-to-strength ratio. Sportswriters and other observers rave about her smooth style. Even when she is tearing up the course, they say, she seems to move in graceful slow motion.

Katie first started climbing in 1994, when she was thirteen. By August 1995, she was ready for the Nationals—a fact she demonstrated by finishing fourth. Although she quickly became a star, Katie says all the attention sometimes can be distracting. She likes to concentrate on the climb itself and not "perform" for other people. Even so, she is now regularly featured in catalogs and magazines.

big bodies necessary to succeed in contact sports such as football or basketball. Today women rock on rock faces, climbing the toughest routes that men climb.

Gyms took climbing indoors. Artificial rock faces are already very popular, although they were invented only in the late 1980s. Practically any hold and combination can be tried on a man-made rock wall. Gym climbers can practice all year without having to travel—or get too cold.

On Ice

Ice climbing can trace its roots back as far as rock climbing. Mountain climbers and Arctic explorers often encountered ice in their journeys. Some climbing historians say that Herschel C. Parker, an American mountaineer, was the first person to snow and ice climb regularly. He made spectacular climbs in the Presidential Range in New Hampshire in the late nineteenth century.

Ice climbing has always been part of "alpining," a winter sport that grew out of mountaineering. Alpining got its start in the European Alps—or did you already figure that out from the name?

Alpiners hike through various mountain, or alpine, areas. They may stay out for a few hours or many days, trekking through the wild. Their hikes can include rock climbing and scrambling. Alpiners may also ski, ice climb, and just plain walk in the course of their trek.

But ice climbing also exists in forms other than alpining. Over the past decade, many climbers have begun to tackle frozen waterfalls and man-made ice.

There are important differences between rock and ice climbing. For one thing, ice climbers use special tools to help them climb.

For another—it's f-f-freezing!

Fortunately, ice climbers rarely if ever feel cold while they climb. They are too busy sweating! That is because ice climbing is hard physical work.

The sports of rock climbing and ice climbing continue to grow and change. New tools and techniques are being developed. These sports are different now from what they were ten years ago. And it is a good bet that they will be even more different ten years from now—extremely different.

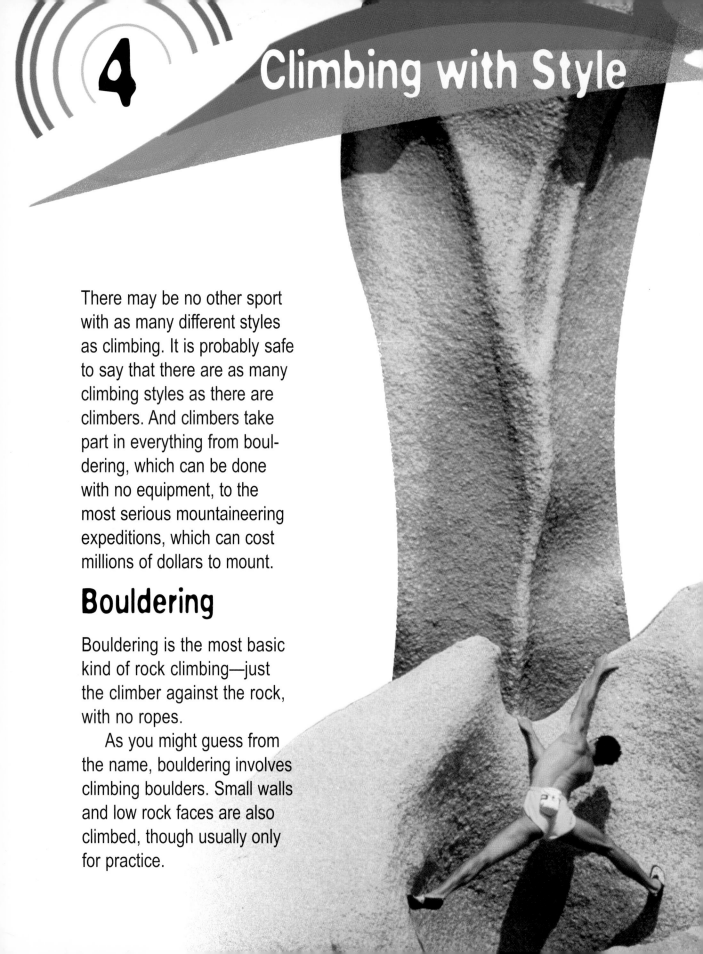

There may be no other sport with as many different styles as climbing. It is probably safe to say that there are as many climbing styles as there are climbers. And climbers take part in everything from bouldering, which can be done with no equipment, to the most serious mountaineering expeditions, which can cost millions of dollars to mount.

Bouldering

Bouldering is the most basic kind of rock climbing—just the climber against the rock, with no ropes.

As you might guess from the name, bouldering involves climbing boulders. Small walls and low rock faces are also climbed, though usually only for practice.

The heights are low enough that safety equipment is not needed. Besides their shoes, the only thing most boulderers take with them is a bag of chalk.

Bouldering is a competitive sport in some countries. It also is used to practice for other kinds of rock climbing. Because it takes place so close to the ground, it is a good way to try difficult moves.

Free Climbing— "Classic" Rock Climbing

In the old days, explorers pitted themselves against the great unknown. Trying to go where no one had ever gone before, they climbed mountains from the ground up. They worked with what nature provided.

Free climbing began the same way. Free climbers always take a rope with them. However, the rope is only for safety. They climb with their hands and feet. They go up thanks to friction, chalk dust, muscle—and sometimes a little attitude.

Even though the path may be well worn, a free climber still sets out from the ground carrying his or her own protection, working with what nature provides.

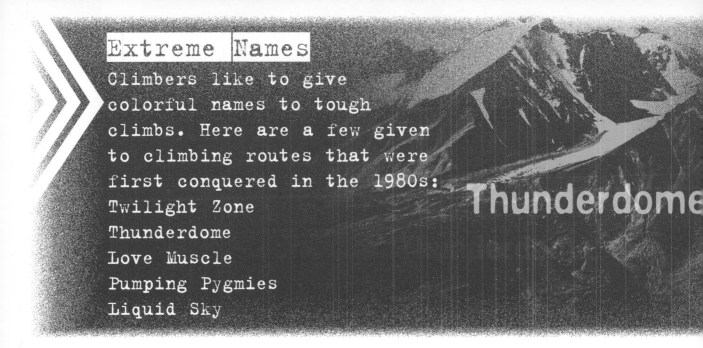

Thunderdome

Sport Climbing

Sport climbers focus on climbing. They do not have to worry about placing anchors or protection as they go; those are already in place. Instead they work on their climbing technique and speed.

Not all sport climbers compete in meets. And not all meets are for sport climbing. But some of the most popular ones—like those at the X Games—are for sport climbing.

Usually two different types of events are held in sport climbing competitions. One is for speed: Fastest to the top wins. In the other, climbers are graded according to the difficult moves they have to perform. Sport climbing can be done on natural or man-made rock faces.

Pulling Plastic

Once, climbers had to go to the mountains. Now the mountains come to them.

Well, almost. The latest innovation in sport climbing is "pulling plastic"—climbing on man-made courses or walls inside a gym. These climbing walls are built especially for climbers. They contain features made of plastic, which is where the nickname comes from. The plastic mimics natural rock formations and cracks.

The walls can be changed easily. Because of this versatility, the same gym can host an easy climb in the morning and a cliffhanger in the afternoon.

Man-made walls and towers helped make climbing into an awesome spectator sport. And unlike mountains, climbing walls can be built anywhere—there is at least one in the middle of New York City.

Soloing

Free and sport climbers use their rope only as safety equipment. They work as part of a team, usually with one other climber.

Some climbers do not use a rope on the climb at all. They climb without protection. This is called soloing.

Soloing on a mountain face is very dangerous. Inexperienced climbers should never attempt it. In fact, only a very few experienced climbers solo.

Ice Climbing

Ice climbing is just like rock climbing—only different.

Ice climbing is different because the climber is going up ice. Instead of using his or her fingers, the climber must rely on tools to pull up. Add in the slippery surface of a frozen waterfall, and things can get frosty.

Competition ice climbing is a very new invention. Just as in rock climbing, competition courses can be either natural or man-made. Ice climbers can free climb or they can sport climb with anchors that are already in the ice.

Man-made ice towers are often extremely difficult to climb. They can be even harder than "real" icy waterfalls. It is not unusual for competitors at a top meet to fall or even fail to reach the top.

Speed climbers are usually top-roped to prevent falls. Their rope is attached to an anchor at the top of the ice wall. That way if they slip, they should fall only a few inches. In the difficulty events, climbers clip into protection as they go, just as rock climbers do.

25

Alpine climbing is a true mountaineer's sport. It combines hiking with ice and rock climbing. It can be more of an endurance test than a marathon running race. Often alpiners spend several nights outdoors during their trek.

Climbing skills are a big part of alpining. But there are some big differences between alpining and technical ice climbing. One is the pack that alpiners carry on their back. Even carrying a light pack changes a climber's balance. They also use different hand tools and may choose different crampons for their feet.

Finally, alpiners face natural hazards that normal climbing protection cannot guard against. Avalanches are just one of Mother Nature's ways of keeping alpiners on the points of their crampons.

Just as ocean liners have lifeboats, most climbers carry a safety system along on the climb. It is often called a belay system. This system consists of rope, "protection," and the connections between the system and the climber.

Teamwork

Traditional free climbing is usually done in teams. Most often, the teams consist of two people—a leader and a follower. The follower is also called the second or belayer.

The lead climber carries a safety rope with him or her. One end of the rope is attached to the climber's

harness. The other trails behind, down to the belayer.

The leader also carries anchors to place in the rock. He or she places these in the rock at several spots along the way. The leader then clips his or her rope to the anchor and continues to climb.

Only one person in a team climbs at a time. The other is "belaying." Belaying works slightly differently depending on which member of the team is doing it. The follower, or second, lets out rope, allowing the leader to climb. The belayer watches the leader carefully. If the leader begins to fall, the follower slides the rope into the belay brake on his or her belt. The brake stops the rope, meaning that the farthest a free climbing leader can fall is twice the distance from the last piece of protection. Depending on where the protection is placed, the fall could be twelve feet or more.

When the second is ready to climb, the leader pulls up the rope to take off any slack. Then he or she puts the rope in the belaying brake. The second starts to climb.

Rating the Rocks

A ratings system is used to rate the difficulty of rock climbs. Classes and numbers are given depending on how tough the climb is. The grading is subjective. That means that two different people might give different ratings to the same climb.

The system starts with an overall rating:

CLASS I = Hiking. A fairly easy walk.

CLASS II = Advanced hiking over rough terrain. Some handholds may be necessary in some places.

CLASS III = "Scrambling" up rocks and boulders is required. Feet and hands will be used in many places for the climb.

CLASS IV = A rope and belay safety system must be used.

CLASS V = Leader protection (anchors) are necessary.

CLASS VI = The climber must use the rope (and/or other devices) to make the climb. The anchors in the rock are necessary for the climb, not just in case of falls. Free and sports climbs are all in Class V. These are also graded according to difficulty. The most popular American grading system for these climbs is called the Yosemite Decimal System. The easiest climb is graded 5.0. The toughest that is still possible without outside help is graded 5.14.

Sometimes the grades above .10 are

subdivided into four more letter grades, with a being the easiest and d the hardest. A climb might be graded .10b, for example, or .12d.

Other times, plus and minus signs are used. For example, a climb might be graded 5.12+. Letters and symbols are not used together, however.

Passing Grades

Most beginning rock climbers tackle 5.4 to 5.7 climbs their first time out. Within a year or so, they are working in the 5.9 to 5.11 category. Generally, climbs of 5.12 and up are attempted only by experts.

Ice Ratings

Like rock climbs, ice climbs are rated according to difficulty. The systems also vary. One popular system ranges from WI 1, which means nearly flat, the kind of walk you might take over your slightly sloped driveway after an ice storm, to WI 7, the truly tough stuff, such as the fierce faces found in the Canadian Rockies. WI 4 and WI 5 designate medium difficulty.

If the second slips, the fall will be only as far as the slack in the rope. Often that is no more than a foot or two. This is one reason why the less experienced climber is usually the second.

On a free climb, the follower retrieves the protection as he or she climbs. This is easier to learn than placing it. But it is not always as easy as it sounds.

Sport climbers use protection that has already been put in place for them. They also can be "top-roped." That means that a permanent anchor is placed at the top of the wall. The rope is also belayed from the bottom. In that case, a climber who slips should fall no more than a few inches. Top-roping is used at many gyms. It also is used in many competitions.

Other than these differences, the belay system is basically the same in free climbing and sport climbing. It is the same whether the climber is top-roped or leads on his or her own. Ice climbers also use a belay system.

Team members communicate by using certain words as they climb. When the follower is ready to climb, he or she may shout up, "Off belay!" The leader then

off belay

takes out the slack in the rope. When his or her belay brake is set, the leader calls down, "On belay."

"Climbing!" shouts the follower, starting up.

Sooner or later, nearly every climber falls. Many of the really great climbers fall frequently, since they are attempting difficult maneuvers. Climbers must learn how to fall very early in their careers.

The right way to fall is with your head up. Your legs and arms should absorb any impact against the rock. Once you stop falling and feel secure, get a grip and go for it again!

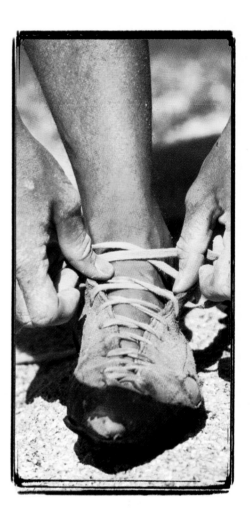

As is true of most sports, climbing requires specific equipment. Like the sport itself, climbing equipment has grown in sophistication and variety. And even though most of the basic skills used in rock and ice climbing are similar, there are important differences in the equipment. Think of it this way: You dress differently to walk along a beach than you would to walk on a glacier.

Rock Shoes

Rock climbers wear shoes specially designed for climbing. All have sticky rubber soles. The rubber usually extends from the heel up over the front toe. This helps improve the shoe's grip on the wall. Compared to hiking boots or even sneakers, the shoes are very light.

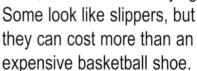

Some look like slippers, but they can cost more than an expensive basketball shoe.

A tight fit is critical. Many climbers wear rock shoes that are a size or two smaller than their regular shoes.

Just like choosing an athletic shoe for basketball or

aerobics, picking a rock shoe is a personal thing. Some climbers like theirs stiff. Stiff shoes are usually a little better for cracks and on steep climbs. The shoes become like miniature climbing pegs. Their stiffness helps hold the climber up.

Other climbers prefer flexible shoes because they allow them to cling to the rock better. In a very flexible shoe, a climber's toes really feel the wall.

Chalk

Chalk helps keep climbers' hands dry. It is not the same kind of chalk teachers use in class. Climbers' chalk is magnesium carbonate, the same kind gymnasts use. The chalk is usually kept in a special chalk bag.

Helmets

Although some climbers do not like to use helmets, they are important on outdoor climbs. Not only do they protect the head during a fall, but they can deflect falling objects.

Rope

Climbing ropes are made of nylon. They are called kermantle ropes and have two parts, a core and a sheath. The core, or center, is constructed to be very strong. The outer part, or sheath, protects against tears and accidental cuts.

Ropes usually are measured according to the metric system. A typical rope would be 50 meters, or about 165 feet, in length. It would be 10 or 11 millimeters in diameter.

Modern climbing ropes come in different

colors and weaves. Their designs make a cool fashion statement.

Because ropes prevent serious injury, they must be handled very carefully. Climbers learn to coil them so that they do not tangle and get dirty. They must be stored properly and inspected often.

Climbing Harness

It is possible to loop a rope around your waist as you climb, but it is not very comfortable. And if the person on the other end of the rope slips . . .

Climbers use special harnesses designed for rope climbing. Harness designs differ, but the basic idea is the same. The harness connects the climber to the safety rope. The rope is attached to the front, where it can be handled easily. Connecting it is called tying on.

Harnesses usually are made out of nylon. They can be plain or wild. It all depends on the climber's personal style.

Anchors

Boats and ships use anchors to stay in place. Climbers use anchors to protect them if they slip. That is why they are sometimes called protection.

There are many kinds of anchors. Each has its own name and use. A nut, or chock, goes into a crack. It is wedged or placed behind a crag to keep it from slipping out. A nut looks like a wedge of metal with a steel cable looping through.

Hexcentrics are nuts whose wedges have six sides. (The prefix hex means "six" in Greek, which is the origin of this word.) They fit into various spots in the rock. Their crazy shapes make them just right for certain tight positions.

The fanciest anchors are cool contraptions that fit into all sorts of strange places. Their official name is spring-loaded cramming devices (SLCDS). The companies that make them often refer to them simply as friends. Their springs and shapes open to keep them in place. They truly are friends for a climber.

Carabiners

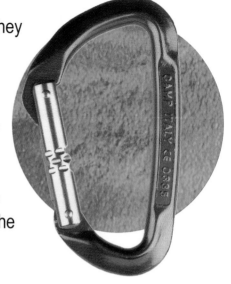

Carabiners look like huge earrings or the metal loop in a keychain. They are actually very important hooks used to hold pieces of equipment together. Some have gates that work like miniature springs to keep the hook closed. Others have screws that do the same thing. Carabiners are also called biners.

Quickdraws

A quickdraw is used to connect the climber's rope to an anchor. As the name indicates, it is designed to be rigged very quickly. A quick-draw is simply two carabiners con-nected by a piece of nylon. Picture two large loop earrings tied to the ends of a nylon strap, or maybe a miniature bungee cord with handy clips on the ends. One biner goes around the safety rope; the other is attached to the anchor. The rope must move freely through the cara-biner. If it does not, the climber will not get very far.

Belay Devices

A belay is a kind of brake applied to the rope. It increases the friction on the rope when someone falls. It is part of the safety system that climbers use. The belay brake is attached to the front of the climber's harness. It does not work automatically. The second must hold the rope and set the brake if the leader slips.

Rock Climbing Fashion

Tight-fitting stretch shorts and not-too-loose T-shirts are the closest thing there is to a standard rock climbing uniform. No baggy pants: Climbers do not want to risk any unnecessary snags that baggy pants might bring. And when you're hanging by your fingers twenty yards above a stream, you don't want to be weighed down.

Many climbers do not wear socks in their climbing shoes. They like the tight feel of the rock through the thin material, since it gives a better grip and feel for the climb.

Ice Climbing Equipment

The exact equipment an ice climber chooses depends on what kind of climbing he or she intends to do. In alpining, ice climbing may be only part of the adventure. Climbers must consider factors such as weight when they choose their tools.

Sport ice climbing usually lasts only a few hours. These technical ice climbers concentrate on the climb itself, whether it is a frozen waterfall or a

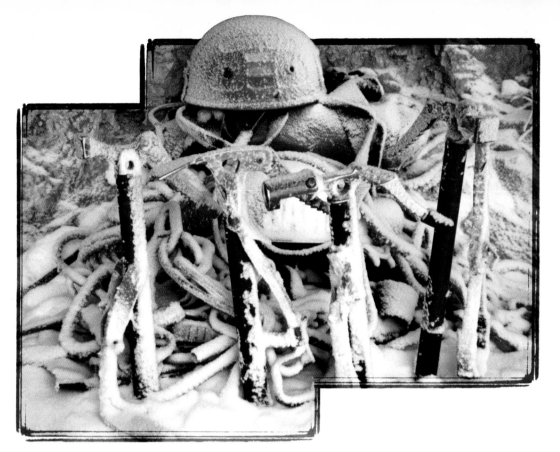

man-made ice tower in a competition. Usually their equipment is made especially for that purpose.

Tools

Rock climbers use their bare fingers as they edge upward. Try that when you are ice climbing, and you may just end up with frostbite.

On a mountain, an alpiner going up a moderate grade often selects a piolet as his or her only hand tool. The piolet is a special type of axe. The head has two parts. The pick is narrow, with teeth that help grip the ice. The back part of the head is called an adze and looks like a miniature hatchet head, twisted sideways. This part is often used to cut holds in the ice. At the top of the head is usually a hole for a wrist leash.

Sport and competition ice climbers use two handheld tools on their climbs. Usually one is an ice hammer. It has a pick side and a hammer or an anvil side. Most people hold hammers in their weaker arm, since the weight of the hammer head helps make their swings stronger.

The other tool many climbers use is an adze or ice axe. The pick ends of

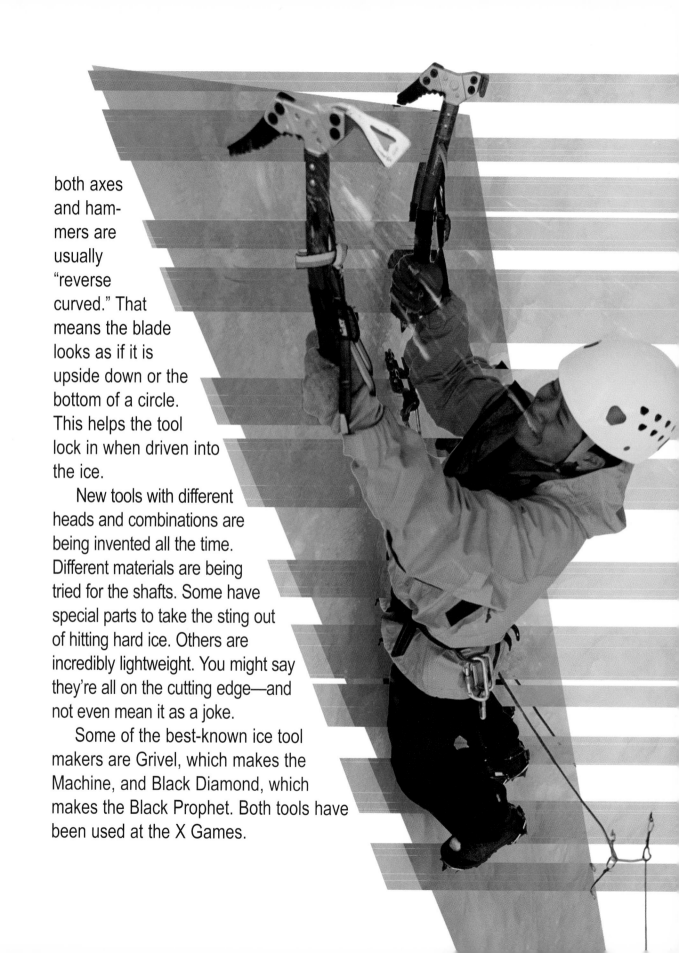

both axes and hammers are usually "reverse curved." That means the blade looks as if it is upside down or the bottom of a circle. This helps the tool lock in when driven into the ice.

New tools with different heads and combinations are being invented all the time. Different materials are being tried for the shafts. Some have special parts to take the sting out of hitting hard ice. Others are incredibly lightweight. You might say they're all on the cutting edge—and not even mean it as a joke.

Some of the best-known ice tool makers are Grivel, which makes the Machine, and Black Diamond, which makes the Black Prophet. Both tools have been used at the X Games.

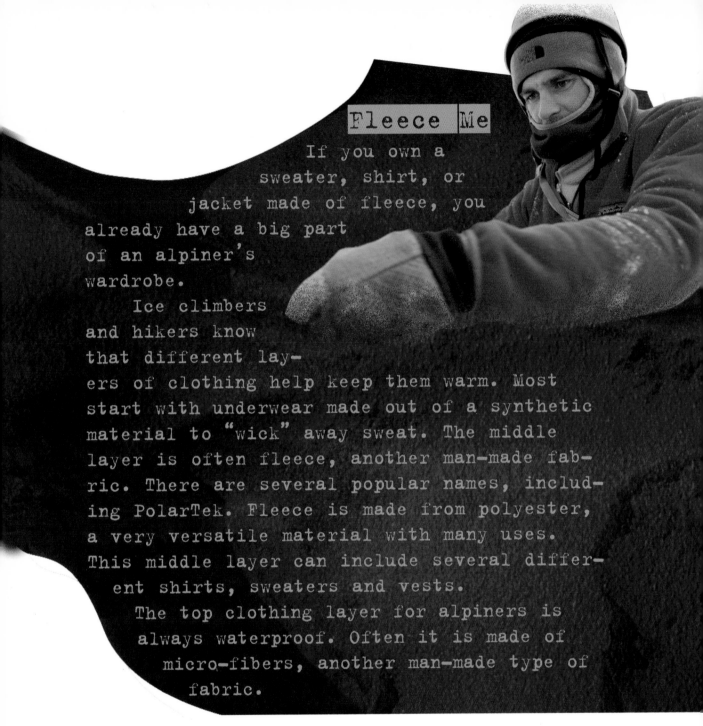

Fleece Me

If you own a sweater, shirt, or jacket made of fleece, you already have a big part of an alpiner's wardrobe.

Ice climbers and hikers know that different layers of clothing help keep them warm. Most start with underwear made out of a synthetic material to "wick" away sweat. The middle layer is often fleece, another man-made fabric. There are several popular names, including PolarTek. Fleece is made from polyester, a very versatile material with many uses. This middle layer can include several different shirts, sweaters and vests.

The top clothing layer for alpiners is always waterproof. Often it is made of micro-fibers, another man-made type of fabric.

Ropes

Ice climbing ropes are specially treated to remain water-repellent. This lessens the chance that they will freeze. They are often called dry ropes.

Boots

Rock climbers wear shoes so light and flexible that they look like slippers. Ice climbers, on the other hand, wear boots that keep their feet warm and dry.

What boots they select depends on what type of climb or adventure they are seeking. Mountain climbers must wear heavy boots that will keep their feet warm and dry. Often they choose double boots. These come with a separate liner that looks like a soft version of the big shoe. The outside boots are usually made of plastic and are waterproof.

Some technical ice climbers prefer light leather boots. Competition ice climbers often make this choice because these boots are lighter. But they are still waterproof.

Crampons

Crampons look like cheese graters with metal spikes on the bottom. They go on the bottom of a climber's boots. They help the climber dig into the ice as he or she goes.

There are two basic kinds: Hinged crampons have separate heel and forward sections. Rigid crampons are all one piece.

Most experienced climbers prefer the hinged type for mountaineering because they are more flexible and comfortable. Rigid crampons are a better choice for steep ice and pillars of frozen water.

Crampons used in ice climbing have front points. These points are like little daggers that a climber can stick into the ice as he or she goes. Competition ice climbers have a choice between one and two front points. Single-point crampons are called monopoints. Experts say that the monopoints are best on hard-water ice, like that used in the X Games. They are easier to control and do not break the ice as much as doubles.

Gloves and Mittens

Are gloves better than mittens in a snowball fight? The debate also rages in ice climbing. The preference is personal, but the aim is always the same: to stay warm and dry.

Harnesses

Ice harnesses loop around the belt and legs. Like rock harnesses, they have a spot for the rope at the front. The loops are almost always bigger than on a rock harness. There is a good reason for this: Ice climbers, especially alpiners, usually wear a lot more clothes than rock climbers!

Anchors

Like rock climbers, ice climbers use a belay system for safety. Their anchors are specially made for ice and snow.

Pickets and deadmen are two types of snow anchors. Pickets look like miniature steel fenceposts. They have a carabiner through them so that they can be attached to a rope. They are two or three feet long and can be pounded into packed snow.

The deadman is for looser snow. Also called a fluke, it looks like a folded piece of metal with a cable looping through it.

Ice protection includes types of anchors that are screwed or pounded into the ice. Round, hollow ice screws allow the ice to escape up through the tube. This lessens the chance of a fracture—and disaster. Some pitons are hollow for the same reason. Pitons are another kind of ice anchor. They also are called "pound-ins" because, duh, they are pounded into the ice.

Ice screws generally are started at an angle. After a gentle tap, the axe or hammer head is used to lever the screw around. At the top of the head is a flange. The flange connects to the belay system, just as rock climbers snap into their protection.

Learning to Climb

Every rock climber has his or her own personal style. There is no one way to cling, claw, or crawl.

Even so, most climbers share some basic moves or techniques. All try to keep three points of contact—hands and feet—on the rock face at all times. If they have a choice, climbers would prefer to let their legs do most of the work, because leg muscles are stronger than arm or hand muscles.

Last but not least, good climbers always look before they climb. They plan where they want to go before they go there. That holds for each move as well as the whole climb.

Feet First: Edging

When you climb a ladder, you usually go toe first. That makes a lot of sense, since you can get the middle of your foot on the rung.

But when you climb rocks, there may not be enough room to get even a whole toe on a hold. That's why climbers use the insides of their feet to climb. This technique is called edging.

Using the inside part of the foot gives a climber more control and stability. It takes advantage of the strongest part of the foot as well as the leg muscles that control it.

You can test the difference yourself by holding on to a stair banister and standing on the bottom step. Place one foot firmly in the middle of the stair. Now experiment with different positions with the other foot. Is your toe stronger than the side of your foot? Which gives you better balance? If you find that edging is the best for you, rock climbing may be in your future.

Smearing Your Way to the Top

The sticky soles of today's climbing shoes make "smearing" a very good technique when the foothold is very small or rounded.

Doing a smear, the climber puts as much of his or her foot as possible on the hold point. The sole is "smeared," or rounded, against the rock, with the ankle rolled outward like a counterweight. It's a little like pasting the foot onto the wall.

Foot Jam

Foot jam is not something you eat with peanut butter. A foot jam is a way of using a crack for a foothold. The heel goes against one side of the crack, and the toes jam against the other. This is a very stable hold. Toe jams are for cracks where only a toe will fit.

A Hand Up

You've probably practiced two or three different climbing grips without even realizing it.

The most basic is the open grip. This is the same grip you might use to pick up a grapefruit—hand spread, with thumb, fingers, and palm sharing the work.

In the cling grip, a climber puts his or her fingertips over a ledge. The cling grip can be strengthened by placing the thumb over the index finger. The thumb tightens the parts that help hold your hand together.

If there is enough room to curl the fingers around the rock, the hand can be extended into a vertical grip, which is much stronger. This grip is also called a hook grip. The hand looks like a hook when the grip is made.

In a pinch grip, the fingers pinch against a small handhold, like a nub the size of a pebble. A finger wrap combines the pinch with a cling. The thumb can help stabilize the grip while pinching at the same time.

Cracking Up

Free climbers often crack up while they are climbing. Not because they are telling jokes or having a nervous breakdown—they use cracks in the rock to climb. They place their fingers or hands inside the openings to pull themselves up or hold their place. These are called jams.

In a finger jam, the fingers are jammed or pushed into a very narrow crack. The little finger is on top, the thumb on the bottom. The more fingers in, the more stable the hold.

A pinkie jam is used in a tiny crack where only the pinkie fits. The pinkie is placed in the crack. The palm is placed on the rock, and the hand is turned gently to increase the grip. This is not considered a very stable hold.

A fist jam is good for larger cracks. The climber makes a fist. Instead of punching the rock, he or she places the fist sideways in the crack, pinkie first. If the crack is a little wider, the fist can be inserted thumb first.

Dynamics

A "dynamic move" is a fancy way of describing a lunge—in which a climber throws his or her body into a new position. "Dynamos" range from short slaps to jumps. The climber tries to use his or her body and position to generate momentum to make the new hold.

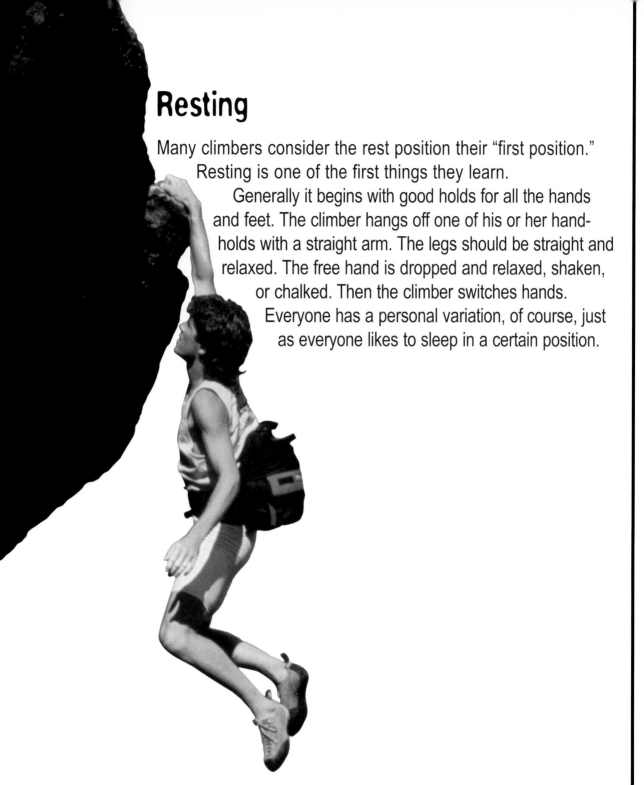

Resting

Many climbers consider the rest position their "first position."
Resting is one of the first things they learn.

Generally it begins with good holds for all the hands
and feet. The climber hangs off one of his or her handholds with a straight arm. The legs should be straight and
relaxed. The free hand is dropped and relaxed, shaken,
or chalked. Then the climber switches hands.

Everyone has a personal variation, of course, just
as everyone likes to sleep in a certain position.

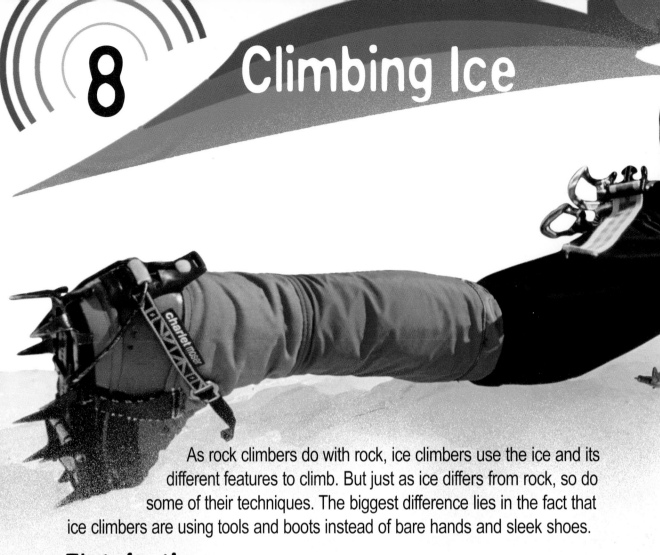

8 Climbing Ice

As rock climbers do with rock, ice climbers use the ice and its different features to climb. But just as ice differs from rock, so do some of their techniques. The biggest difference lies in the fact that ice climbers are using tools and boots instead of bare hands and sleek shoes.

Flat-footing

Flat-footing usually is used for level ice. It also is good for gentle and medium slopes, ones that you might sleigh or even ski on. Alpiners use this style a lot. The basic idea is to have all ten bottom points of the crampons in contact with the ice whenever possible, with small variations depending on the slope.

Walking on flat or nearly flat surfaces, climbers move slowly and deliberately. The feet are a little farther apart than in normal walking. Climbers stamp their feet flat to make sure that the crampon points press down well.

On a gentle slope, flat-footers turn into ducks. Or at least they use a fowlish way to walk. They move their feet farther apart and waddle forward. Taking short steps and keeping your weight balanced is very important in the duck walk.

On a steep slope, one basic style of flat-footing is like walking sideways. The side of the climber's body faces the top. As the climber goes up the slope, he or she always tries to keep the soles of the feet even against the hill. By rolling the ankle out away from the slope, the bottom crampons move into the proper position. The climber can go up a short distance sideways or walk in diagonals as if zigzagging up the hill.

Flat-footing is a basic technique, but even the waddle is not easy the first time you do it. Climbers must lift and place their feet carefully. If they try to slide or shuffle, they could break an ankle. When climbers flat-foot, their leg muscles get a serious workout.

Toes First

Very steep slopes and vertical ice call for front-pointing. Here the crampons toe into the ice. The front points should go into the ice exactly level. Short kicks are the key. Experts concentrate on control and keeping their boot heels down.

Hand Tools

Hand tools are used with both crampon techniques. Again, there are different styles depending on the slope and type of ice, as well as the athlete.

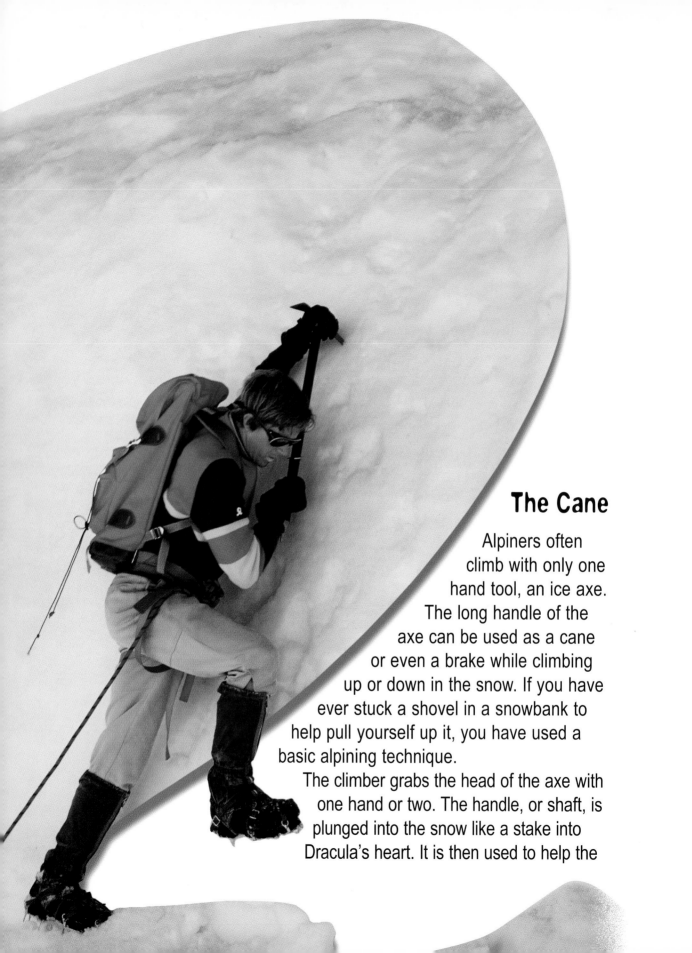

The Cane

Alpiners often climb with only one hand tool, an ice axe. The long handle of the axe can be used as a cane or even a brake while climbing up or down in the snow. If you have ever stuck a shovel in a snowbank to help pull yourself up it, you have used a basic alpining technique.

The climber grabs the head of the axe with one hand or two. The handle, or shaft, is plunged into the snow like a stake into Dracula's heart. It is then used to help the alpiner move up or down. Gripping the top with one hand is called the cane, or *piolet canne,* a French term. The two-handed move, usually for steeper slopes, is a *piolet manche.*

Just Axin'

Sport and technical ice climbers go up vertical ice. Because of this, they use their hand tools constantly. They usually use two, an axe and a hammer. The tools are an extension of their hands as they flash upward.

Swinging an ice tool is a little like using a hammer to nail a board overhead. A good swing starts with the arm extended in front of the climber. The head of the tool is about halfway through the arc the climber will make. The climber swings his or her arm backward and then forward in one easy motion extending into the rock. The shoulder helps drive the axe, while the elbow acts as a pivot. Because it is vital to put the axe point exactly where the climber wants it, control is more important than strength.

Emergency Brake

Alpiners practice a technique known as self-arrest. It is not something they do when they break the law. Instead it is a

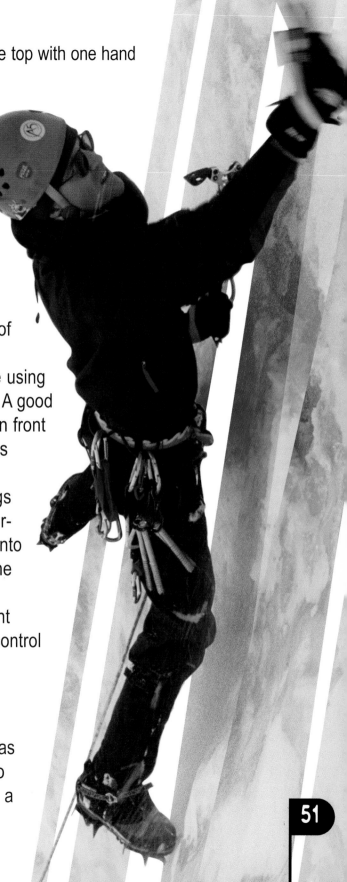

way to stop themselves if they fall down a mountain.

The falling climber holds the ice axe across his or her chest. The axe head is closest to the climber's head. He or she then arches the body from the shoulders to his knees. Finally the climber rolls onto the pick, using it as a brake. The climber must put his or her weight on the pick end. Otherwise the handle could act as a pole vault, making matters even worse.

Monkeying Around

The monkey hang is a popular method of getting over a bulge in the ice. The feet are "walked" up the ice face while the rest of the body remains in place. One tool is loosened, and then the body is lifted. The loosened tool goes upward and is planted. The second tool follows. Then the climber can then start the process all over again.

Beginning rock climbers, especially young climbers looking for instruction, can start in a local gym that has a rock climbing wall. Most offer classes or one-on-one instruction for beginners. These classes are a good way to learn the basics. They help students and beginners work on exercises to improve strength and agility. Plus they can introduce newcomers to more experienced climbers.

Most gyms supply climbing shoes and a harness as well as the rope. Some gyms and programs have age requirements or require young beginners to have their parents' permission before climbing.

Even so, you can start sport climbing at a very young age. The Junior Competition Climbing Association (JCCA) sponsors competitions and rates climbers nineteen years of age and younger. The youngest division is for kids under twelve. National champions are selected for a Junior World Team.

There are many formal competitions in rock and ice climbing. Local gyms and clubs regularly hold small meets. These usually feature speed and difficulty events. Bouldering, redpoints, and on-site competitions are also popular.

Climbing People

Although only a teenager, Shena Sturman is a member of the U.S. Climbing Team, which competes in world events. Sturman had been involved in the sport for less than four years when she made the team. "Do what you want in climbing," she says, "not what other people want you to do." Shena climbs three or four days a week instead of training. "I just climb," she says.

Colder than Cool
Freezing Up

Ice climbing competitions such as the X Games usually rely on man-made walls of ice. The ice is cut and sculpted by workers right before the competition. The goal is to make it seem like a natural waterfall. Many of the ice structures freeze simply because it is cold outside. But at the 1998 Winter X Games, liquid nitrogen was used to freeze the ice into a wall eighteen inches thick.

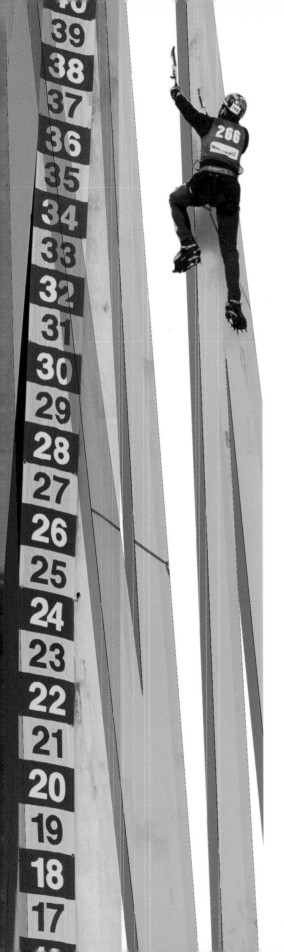

Rock and ice climbers can compete in regional and national events. If they are good enough to make the U.S. Climbing Team or another national-level squad, they can go on to world competition. The best athletes also take part in special events such as the ESPN X Games. Youth is not a barrier. Some of the best sport climbers in the world are teenagers. Katie Brown, for example, became a star at fourteen.

There is much more to climbing than sports competitions, of course. Many novices who begin in the gym soon move outdoors. Because modern outdoor free climbing usually is done in two-person teams, beginners start as followers, or seconds. Working with an experienced climber, novices generally are very safe, even on a high climb. After gaining more experience, they can take over and lead a climb.

Leading takes special skills. The leader is responsible for choosing the route. He or she also places the protection.

Alpining is a very demanding sport that includes climbing and other skills. One way to get a taste of alpining is to join a hiking or camping group. Many have hikes and other programs for beginners. For decades, young men and women have joined the Boy Scouts or Girl Scouts as well as other youth organiza- tions to learn the basics of hiking, climbing, and camping.

As far as it has come in the past two or three decades, climbing remains a young sport. It still comes down to one person working with his or her body against gravity. It is sweat versus rock and ice. From the highest to the lowest level, climbers are always competing with themselves, trying to push the limits.

That is what makes climbing so extreme.

Climbing People

When a scrambling accident cost him the use of his legs, Mark Wellman did not give up his love of the rocks. Demonstrating that the physically challenged can achieve in even the toughest environments, Mark scaled the 3,000-foot wall known as The Shield on El Capitan Mountain in California. He described the climb as "seven thousand chin-ups."

X-Planations

abseil   The German word for "rappel." It means "to lower yourself with a rope."

airtime   A long fall. As in, "I slipped and did some serious airtime."

anchors   Protection placed in the ice or rock face for the belaying system. Can be permanent or removable.

barndoor   A climber who has lost his or her grip and is swinging on the rope.

belay   Holding one end of the safety rope. One person belays while another climbs. If the other person falls, the belayer helps stop the fall with a belaying brake. When the leader climbs, the follower, or belayer, feeds rope through the belay device. "Belay" also is used to describe the device.

Camalot   A trade name for a trigger-activated cramming device or a special kind of anchor.

carabiner   A metal loop used for attaching different pieces of equipment. Found on some types of anchors and quickdraws. Also called "biners." They have different types of gates, allowing the carabiner to be attached to a rope or other item.

chalk   Really magnesium carbonate, not the stuff your teacher uses to write on the blackboard. It is used to improve the climber's grip.

cramming device   A special type of anchor that springs out and holds itself in place. Also called a trigger-activated cramming device.

crux The hardest part of a climb.

drytooling When ice climbers find it necessary to use their tools and crampons on bare rock.

flash To successfully climb up a face without falling.

friend A trade name for a trigger-activated cramming device or a special kind of anchor.

lock off Hanging by the arms to relieve leg and other muscles while climbing.

mank Used as an adjective to describe an older bolt that might not hold, as in, "Could be mank; I wouldn't trust it."

nut A small wedge-shaped anchor that includes a steel wedge with a steel wire and is used as protection.

on-sight Climbing a new route for the first time, without extra help. As in, "We hadn't seen the face before, so we on-sighted it."

protection The anchors and other items that hold the rope in place.

rack The collection of protection that the leader brings. The word can also refer to the belt or holder where the protection is kept during the climb.

rappel To lower yourself with a rope. Climbers can rappel down a face before or after a climb, depending on where they started from. Rappelling is also an activity separate from climbing.

redpoint A flash after practicing a route a few times. A redpoint usually represents a personal best for a climber.

rock jock A sport climber. Other terms include "wall rats," "rock hounds," and "hang dogs." Depending on who uses them, they may or may not be compliments.

route The path of a climb up a rock face or a manmade wall.

technical climbing This term can mean slightly different things to different people. Its most basic meaning is any climbing done with a rope. Usually, it means free climbing with a belay system for protection. Technical ice climbing means the same thing in reference to ice climbing.

top-roping A style of climbing in which the rope is anchored at the top of the climb. Because the anchor is always in place, the climb is very safe, and falls are very short. Top-roping is often used in gyms and in practice.

whip The end of a long fall. It describes what can happen to the climber.

Climbing Organizations

The Access Fund
P.O. Box 17010
Boulder, CO 80308
Works to keep climbing areas open.

American Alpine Club
(303) 384-0110
Works on alpine issues.

American Mountain Guides Association
(303) 271-0984
An association of guides that provides training, publications, and conferences.

American Sport Climbers Federation
(888) ASCF-ROX
Regulates climbing competitions.

Junior Competition Climbing Association (JCCA)
P.O. Box 19145
Portland, Oregon 97280-0145
For climbers under twenty-one.

The Mountaineers
300 Third Avenue West
Seattle, WA 98119
(888) 788-5222
Club dedicated to mountaineering in the Northwest.

Web Sites

http://www.amga.org (the American Mountain Guides Association)
http://www.climbnet.com/ascf/index/html
http://www.climbnet.comindex/html (has a lot of useful links)
http://www.espn.sportszone.com/extreme/climbing/index.html
http://www.juniorclimbing.org
http://www.outdoor.com
http://www.outdoorlink.com/accessfund
http://www.texasmountaineers.org (a good local site with a lot of links)

Extreme Reading

Books

Cinnamon, Jerry. *Climbing Rock and Ice—Learning the Vertical Dance.* Camden, ME:Ragged Mountain Press (McGraw-Hill), 1994.

Goddard, Dale, and Udo Neumann. *Performance Rock Climbing.* Mechanicsburg, PA: Stackpole Books, 1993.

Graydon, Don, and Kurt Hanson, eds. *Mountaineering—The Freedom of the Hills.* Seattle, WA: The Mountaineers, 1997.

Johnston, Turlough, and Madeleine Halldén. *Rock Climbing Basics.* Mechanicsburg, PA: Stackpole Books, 1997.

Raleigh, Duane. *Ice:Tools and Techniques.* Carbondale, CO: Elk Mountain Press, 1995.

Waterman, Laura, and Guy Waterman. *Yankee Rock & Ice.* Mechanicsburg, PA: Stackpole Books, 1996.

Watts, Phil. *Rock Climbing.* Champaign, IL: Human Kinetics, 1996.

Magazines

Climbing
1101 Village Road, Suite LL-1-B
Carbondale, CO 81623
(303) 963-9449

Rock & Ice
P.O. Box 3595
Boulder, CO 80307
(303) 499-8410

Index

Credits

About the Author

Jeremy Roberts is the pen name of Jim DeFelice. Jim often uses this name when he writes for young readers, which he tries to do as much as he can. Besides extreme sports books on sky-diving and climbing for Rosen Publishing, Jim's recent nonfiction includes biographies on King Arthur and Joan of Arc. He has written several installments in the *Eerie, Indiana,* series and a bunch of horror stories. His books for adults include techno-thrillers and a historical trilogy. Jim lives with his wife and son in a haunted farmhouse in upstate New York. His latest hobby is learning to fly airplanes, not jumping from them—but for some reason his flight instructor still calls him "The Rock."

Photo Credits

Series Design

Oliver Halsman Rosenberg

Layout

Laura Murawski

Consulting Editor

Amy Haugesag